W9-AJT-307

Date: 01/18/12

J 597.9 MIL
Miller, Ruth,
Reptiles /

Reptiles

Ruth Miller

Raintree
Chicago, Illinois

© 2005 Raintree
Published by Raintree, a division of Reed Elsevier Inc.
Chicago, Illinois
Customer Service 888-363-4266
Visit our website at www.raintreelibrary.com

For information, address the publisher:
Raintree, 100 N. LaSalle, Suite 1200, Chicago, IL 60602

Produced for Raintree by
White-Thomson Publishing Ltd.

Consultant: Dr. Rod Preston-Mafham
Page layout by Tim Mayer
Photo research by Morgan Interactive Ltd.

Originated by Dot Gradations Ltd.
Printed in China by WKT Company Limited

09 08 07 06
10 9 8 7 6 5 4 3 2

Library of Congress Cataloging-in-Publication Data
Miller, Ruth, 1936-
    Reptiles / Ruth Miller.
        p. cm. -- (Animal kingdom)
Includes bibliographical references (p.   ) and index.
Contents: Reptiles -- Ectothermy -- Reptile classification --
Tortoises
and turtles -- Snakes -- The cobra -- The monitors.
    ISBN 1-4109-1052-0 (library binding : hardcover) -- ISBN 1-
4109-1348-1 (pbk.)
    1. Reptiles--Juvenile literature. [1. Reptiles.] I. Title. II.
Series: Miller, Ruth, 1936-   Animal kingdom.
    QL644.2.M49 2005
    597.9--dc22
                                                2003024893

Acknowledgments

The publisher would like to thank the following for permission
to reproduce copyright materials : Corbis pp.18, 60 top, 61, 62;
Digital Vision **Title page**, pp.10 bottom, 37 top, 58, 60 bottom,
64; Ecoscene pp.10 top (Sally Morgan), 16–17, 17 top (John
Pitcher), 20 bottom (Luc Hosten), 21 (Reinhard Dirscherl),
22 (Edward Bent), 24 top (Robert Baldwin), 24 bottom
(Brandon Cole /V&W), 29 top (Frank Blackburn), 41 top (Sally
Morgan), 43 top, 45 top (Wayne Lawler), 52 bottom (Chinch
Gryniewicz), 54–55 (Robert Baldwin), 55 bottom (Joel Creed),
56 (Stephen Coyne), 57 bottom (Matthew Bolton);
Ecoscene/Papilio **contents page** (Dennis Johnson), pp.15
bottom (Jack Milchanowski), 25 (Robert Pickett), 30 (Paul
Franklin), 39 bottom (Dennis Johnson), 45 bottom (Clive
Druett), 58–59 (Dennis Johnson); Nature Picture Library
pp.6 top (Jean Roche), 6 bottom and 7 (Jurgen Freund),
9 (Mike Wilkes), 12 top (Anup Shah), 13 bottom (David Shale),
14 (Hans Christoph Kappel), 19 (John Cancalosi), 23 bottom
(Bernard Castelein), 26 bottom (Pete Oxford), 27 (Doug
Wechsler), 28 bottom (John Cancalosi), 31 bottom (Peter
Blackwell), 34 (Constantinos Petrinos), 35 top (Morley Read),
36 top (John Downer), 48–49 (Michael Pitts), 50 (Anup Shah),
51 top (Peter Blackwell), 51 bottom (Peter Scoones), 52 top
(Richard Kirby), 53 (Anup Shah), 55 top (Bruce Davidson),
57 top Jurgen Freund; NHPA pp.4–5 (James Carmichael),
5 bottom (Daniel Heuclin), 7 top (Anthony Bannister), 11 top
(William Patton), 13 top (Stephen Dalton), 15 top (Daniel
Heuclin), 17 bottom (James Carmichael), 20 top (Hellio and
Van Ingen), 23 top (Daniel Heuclin), 26 top (ANT), 32 bottom
(Anthony Bannister), 33 bottom (Rod Planck), 35 bottom
(Anthony Bannister), 36–37 (Daniel Heuclin), 38 bottom,
(James Carmichael), 39 top (Daniel Heuclin), 41 bottom (James
Carmichael), 42 and 44 (Stephen Dalton), 46, 47 top (Daniel
Heuclin), 47 bottom (Daniel Zupanc), 49 bottom (Jonathan and
Angela Scott); Photodisc pp.5, 8 left, 28 top, 31 top, 32–33, 40,
43 bottom; Tudor Photography p.8 bottom.

Cover photograph of young Nile crocodiles reproduced with
permission of NHPA (Martin Harvey)

Every effort has been made to contact copyright holders of any
material reproduced in this book. Any omissions will be rectified
in subsequent printings if notice is given to the publisher.

The paper used to print this book comes from sustainable
resources.

Contents

INTRODUCING REPTILES   4

REPTILE BEHAVIOR AND LIFE CYCLE   6

Life Cycle of a Snake   8

Keeping Warm   10

Movement   12

Reptile Senses   14

REPTILIAN ORDERS   16

Reptiles of the Past   18

Tortoises and Turtles   20

The Green Turtle   24

Tuataras   26

Snakes   28

Boas and Pythons   30

Colubrids   32

Elapids   34

The Cobra   36

Vipers   38

Lizards   40

Chameleons and Iguanas   42

Geckos and Skinks   44

Monitors   46

The Komodo Dragon   48

Crocodiles and Alligators   50

The Nile Crocodile   52

REPTILES UNDER THREAT   54

Protecting Reptiles   56

CLASSIFICATION   58

Reptile Evolution   60

GLOSSARY   62

FURTHER INFORMATION   63

INDEX   64

Introducing Reptiles

Reptiles belong to a large group of animals called vertebrates. These are animals with backbones. Other vertebrates include mammals, fish, birds, and amphibians. Scientists believe that reptiles evolved from amphibians. Most reptiles lay eggs and have four limbs and dry, scaly skins. Reptiles are found all over the world except the Arctic and the Antarctic. They are more common in hot, dry regions.

Cold-blooded animals

Reptiles are ectothermic, or cold-blooded, animals. This means they cannot keep their internal body temperatures constant by generating heat themselves. Reptiles depend on the temperature of their environments to keep their bodies warm. Mammals and birds are different because they can generate heat inside their bodies, and their body temperatures do not vary significantly.

Classification

Living organisms are classified, or organized, according to how closely related one organism is to another. The basic group in classification is the species. For example, human beings belong to the species *Homo sapiens*. A species is a group of individuals that are similar to each other and that can interbreed with one another. Species are grouped together into genera (singular: genus). A genus may contain a number of species that share some features. *Homo* is the human genus. Genera are grouped together in families, the families are grouped into orders, and the orders are grouped into classes. Classes are grouped together into phyla (singular: phylum), and finally, the phyla are grouped into kingdoms. Kingdoms are the largest groups. Reptiles belong to the animal kingdom.

▼ Geckos are common, small lizards found in tropical and subtropical habitats. Most are nocturnal and have large eyes with vertical pupils. Day geckos, like this gold dust day gecko, are usually brightly colored.

This means that mammals and birds can be independent of the temperature of their surroundings. Reptiles cannot survive for long at very hot or very cold temperatures.

Egg layers

Most reptiles lay eggs, but some give birth to live young. Nearly all reptiles lay their eggs or give birth to their young on land. Reptilian eggs have hard or leathery shells to protect the developing embryo inside. The young that hatch from the eggs are fully formed and look like their parents.

Scaly bodies

Most reptiles have elongated bodies and long tails. The body is covered with waterproof, horny scales that protect the reptile and prevent it from drying up. Most reptiles have two pairs of limbs, and each limb usually has five toes with claws. The limbs may be adapted for climbing, running, or swimming. Snakes and some lizards do not have limbs.

The scaly skin is waterproof and enables the lizard to survive in dry habitats.

The limbs are positioned directly under the body, raising it from the ground.

▲ This lizard shows the typical reptile features of scaly skin, four limbs, an elongated body, and a long tail.

◄ Turtles and tortoises form a group of reptiles with short, broad bodies surrounded by tough shells. They have horny beaks instead of teeth.

Reptile Behavior and Life Cycle

Most reptiles live on land. Their life cycle is different from that of the amphibians from which they evolved. Amphibians have to return to water to lay their eggs, and they can live only in damp places so that their skin does not dry out. Reptiles have thick, waterproof skins that do not dry out or let water in. They can live in a greater range of habitats.

▲ Reptiles lay their eggs on land, often burying them in soft sand. The eggs of most reptile species have leathery shells that allow the exchange of gases for respiration.

Mating and laying eggs

Mating occurs when the reptiles become mature. Some reptiles show courtship behavior to attract females before mating. Males may fight each other for territory or for the right to mate with certain females. Some lizards change color or make sounds to show that they are ready to mate. Fertilization of the eggs takes place inside the body of the female.

Egg-laying reptiles lay their eggs on land. Most eggs are laid in nests, underground, or in piles of rotting vegetation where the temperature does not vary much. The warmer the temperature, the faster the embryo develops. However, the temperature must not get too high. For reptiles living in temperate climates, egg-laying occurs in the summer months. In some reptiles, such as marine turtles, the surrounding temperature determines whether the eggs develop into males or females.

▼ Young lizards break through the tough egg shells using their egg teeth.

▲ All reptiles molt as they grow. In snakes, the skin is shed in one piece. Other reptiles, such as the gecko shown here, shed their skin in pieces.

Most reptiles do not take any interest in their eggs or young. Some snakes do coil around the eggs to protect and warm them, and crocodiles help the young hatch and carry them to the water. Most eggs are left unattended, and the young fend for themselves after hatching. Reptilian young hatch fully formed as miniature adults.

Tortoises, turtles, tuataras, amphisbaenians (worm lizards), crocodiles, and alligators are oviparous, which means they lay eggs. Many snakes and lizards are also oviparous, but in some species the eggs are kept warm inside the female's body. These species are called ovoviviparous. Other species, such as the Cuban wood snake and the long-tailed skink, are viviparous. This means they give birth to live young.

Amazing facts

- The green anole, a lizard found in the United States, has a bright pink throat fan that it uses to signal to rival males and potential mates.
- Female crocodilians stay with their young for several months after hatching.

Molting

Most reptiles molt, or shed their outer skin, as they grow. In snakes, the outer skin comes off in one piece, but in all other reptiles it comes off in flakes. Reptiles continue to grow even after they have become mature. They need to molt to replace old skin, which otherwise would become too stretched and tear.

Life Cycle of a Snake

Most snakes lay eggs but do not show any parental care. The eggs are laid in batches called clutches that may contain up to 100 eggs. Each egg has a soft, leathery shell surrounding the embryo and the yolk. The yolk contains all the food the embryo needs to develop into a young snake. The water and oxygen needed by the embryo can pass through the shell into the egg.

Incubating eggs

The rate at which the eggs develop depends on the temperature of the surroundings. The warmer the temperature, the faster the embryo will grow and so the incubation period will be shorter. Snake species that live in temperate climates mate soon after they emerge from their period of winter hibernation. Their eggs are laid in the warm summer months. Snakes that live in tropical climates have a longer breeding season due to the higher temperatures.

Eggs may be laid in piles of leaves or holes in the ground. Some snakes lay their eggs in rotting vegetation where the temperature is higher because of the heat produced by bacteria by breaking down the plant remains.

▶ This adult monocle cobra shows the main characteristics of snakes: a long, thin body covered in scales, no limbs, no eyelids, and no external ears.

▲ As a snake grows, it sheds its skin at intervals. This happens throughout the life of the snake. The skin is shed in one piece.

From hatching to adulthood

When a young snake is ready to hatch, it breaks out of its shell using the egg tooth. This is used to make a hole in the shell. The eggs in one clutch are usually all ready to hatch at about the same time. The young are fully developed and look like a smaller version of their parents. As soon as they hatch, the young snakes have to look after themselves and find food. Growth is rapid, but it takes from one to five years, depending on the species, for snakes to become adult and ready to mate. As they grow, they molt. Young snakes molt more frequently than the adults.

In some snake species, the young are born alive. This has the advantage of the young developing inside the mother's body and being kept at an even temperature, as well as being protected from predators. Usually, viviparous species have fewer young than their egg-laying relatives.

Amazing snake facts

- When they are born, a young rattlesnake does not have a rattle in its tail. Instead, there is a small, buttonlike structure at the end of the tail where a new section of the rattle develops after each molt.
- No male Brahminy blind snakes have ever been found. The females lay eggs without mating. This process is known as parthenogenesis.

▼ Pythons are different from other reptiles because they look after their eggs. The female python coils around the clutch and guards them. This also keeps them at an even temperature.

Keeping Warm

Reptiles are ectothermic, which means they cannot generate enough heat inside their bodies. They have to get heat from their environment to keep them at a suitable, constant temperature.

A reptile's activity is determined by the temperature of its surroundings. Most reptiles live in areas where the daytime temperature is 86 to 104 °F (30to 40°C), so many species are found in tropical and subtropical regions of the world. Reptiles that live in temperate regions usually retreat to burrows and hibernate during the coldest months. In deserts, the temperatures during the day may become too hot. So the reptiles hide in underground burrows and may become inactive for the hottest periods of the year. This condition is known as estivation.

▲ If the surface of the sand becomes too hot, this gecko raises its body and tail off the ground to reduce contact.

◀ Sand lizards absorb heat from the ground in the early morning. They press the lower surfaces of their bodies against the sand. Their body temperatures rise rapidly.

Basking and cooling down

Lizards tend to bask in the early morning sun to warm up after a cold night. When the lizard's body temperature has reached about 85 °F (30 °C), it actively searches for food and water. During the middle part of the day, the temperature may become too high, and the lizard takes cover in the shade or burrows underground. In the late afternoon, the lizard may have another period of activity before the temperature drops and becomes too cool.

If conditions become too hot, reptiles try to find shade or other ways of cooling down. Aquatic or semiaquatic reptiles, those that live in or near water, move back into the water. Reptiles that live on land hide under rocks, in burrows, or bury themselves in the sand. Some snakes, lizards, and crocodilians open their mouths wide. This allows water to evaporate from their mouths and cools them down.

▲ Marine iguanas feed on seaweed in the cold waters off the Galapagos Islands. They spend a lot of time basking on rocks to warm up.

Amazing facts

- In a 24-hour period, a desert lizard spends about 10 percent of its time basking to warm up and 34 percent of its time hunting for food and water. The rest of the time, it is either too hot or too cold for the lizard to be active.
- Tuataras are tolerant of cold conditions and can stay active at 50 °F (10 °C).

Color change

Many reptiles, particularly lizards, can change the color of their skin. This color change is brought about by the effect of light or temperature on special cells in the skins. Dark colors absorb heat more easily. The skins of some lizards are dark in the early morning when it is cold and become paler as they warm up during the day.

Movement

Most reptiles have four sturdy limbs that may be used for walking and running on land or climbing trees. However, some lizards and all snakes have no limbs. They use their scales and muscles to move from one place to another.

◄ Like most reptiles, this crocodile sways from side to side as it moves.

Walking, climbing, and swimming

The limbs of reptiles, like those of amphibians, are attached to the sides of the body. The feet are bent forward at right angles to rest on the ground. When most reptiles run, their legs move in diagonally opposite pairs. In lizards, the front right and back left limbs go forward first, followed by the front left and back right limbs. This makes the body sway from side to side.

Some reptiles, such as the chameleon, have adapted to climbing trees. They usually have well-developed claws for gripping the tree bark and branches. Many geckos have wide pads on the ends of their toes, with thousands of tiny bristles underneath so that they can move quickly over smooth, vertical surfaces.

The limbs of marine turtles are modified into flippers for swimming. The front flippers are bigger than the hind ones and are used like oars to propel the turtle through the water. The hind limbs are used for steering. These turtles do not have claws, so they find it difficult to move around on land when they come ashore to lay their eggs.

▼ This is the nearest a lizard gets to flying. The flying dragon uses the flaps of skin along the sides of its body to glide from one branch to another.

Slithering

Snakes and lizards with no limbs move in a variety of ways. In serpentine movements, the animals move from side to side in a series of waves. The waves are caused when muscles contract or tighten along the body. Some snakes with heavy bodies, such as boas and pythons, use the scales on their bellies to grip the ground so that they creep forward like caterpillars. This type of movement is used for burrowing and moving forward in a straight line when stalking prey. Accordianlike movements, in which the snake pulls itself forward by bunching and extending its muscles, are used for climbing, crossing smooth surfaces, and burrowing.

Flying

Reptiles cannot fly, but some can glide. The flying dragon has flaps of skin along the sides of its body that act like a parachute when opened. The flying gecko has webbed feet and flaps of skin along the sides of its body.

Amazing facts

- The fastest speed recorded for a reptile on land is 22 miles (35 kilometers) per hour by a spiny-tailed iguana from Central America.
- Some sea turtles can reach speeds of up to 19 miles (30 kilometers) per hour.
- The web-footed gecko has flaps of skin between its toes to help it run across loose sand without sinking.

◀ Sidewinders are snakes that can move rapidly across loose sand. They lift parts of their bodies clear off the ground and then use the tracks to push themselves forward.

Reptile Senses

Reptiles have well-developed senses, and some have sense organs not found in any other animal group. Many reptiles have good vision and a good sense of smell, but their hearing is generally poor.

Reptile vision

Many reptiles have large, prominent eyes. In diurnal reptiles, those that are active during the day, the pupils of the eyes are round. Nocturnal reptiles, which hunt at night, have vertical, slitlike pupils.

Eyelid structure varies among reptiles. Turtles, tortoises, crocodilians, and most other reptiles have upper and lower eyelids that can open and shut. Some snakes and lizards have transparent eyelids that are joined to form a complete covering over the front of the eye.

In the crocodilians and tuataras, there is a third eyelid, called a nictitating membrane. This is a transparent fold of skin that moves sideways across the front of the eye. It protects and cleans the front part of the eye.

Tuataras and some lizards have a third, or median, eye beneath the skin on the top of the head. This is not a true eye because it does not form images, but it is sensitive to light. Some people think the median eye might measure the length of the daylight and control daily or seasonal activities.

▶ A chameleon can swivel each eye separately from the other. It can look backward and forward at the same time. Therefore, it is possible to hunt for food while watching for predators.

Amazing facts

- The special heat sensitive organs of pit vipers and boas can detect temperature changes as small as 0.004 °F (0.002 °C).
- Most reptiles can hear low-pitched noises. Snakes have a simple inner ear and can only detect vibrations that pass through their jawbones into this inner ear.

▲ A pit viper has a pair of pits containing heat sensors in the skin between the eyes and the nostrils. The pits point forward. By moving the head from side to side, the snake can track and stalk its warm-blooded prey.

Sensing heat

Pit vipers, boas, and pythons have heat sensors that can detect small changes in the temperature of their surroundings. This helps the snakes catch warm-blooded prey, such as small mammals. It helps them keep their own bodies at a suitable temperature by signaling when to move to a warmer or cooler place. Pit vipers have heat sensors in pits between the eyes and the nostrils, but boas and pythons have heat pits along their upper and lower lips.

Forked tongues

When a snake or lizard flicks its forked tongue out of its mouth, it picks up chemical substances in the air. As the snakes draws its tongue back into the mouth, the tips of the forks enter special pouches in the roof of the mouth, called Jacobson's organs. Here, sensory cells identify chemicals that provide information about food, possible mates, or enemies.

▲ Snakes and lizards continually flick their forked tongues in and out to get information about their surroundings.

Reptilian Orders

There are four different reptile orders: the chelonians (tortoises and turtles), the tuataras, the squamates (snakes, lizards, and amphisbaenians), and the crocodilians (alligators and crocodiles).

Chelonians

Chelonians have hard shells that completely cover their soft bodies. They do not have teeth, but they have horny beaks instead. Chelonians are divided into two groups according to the way in which the head is withdrawn into the shell. The turtles in the most primitive group have long necks and tuck their heads sideways into their shells. Most chelonians have shorter necks that are drawn straight back beneath their shells.

Tuataras

Tuataras are more closely related to the squamates than they are to the chelonians or to the crocodilians. There is only one family (Sphenodontidae), and these reptiles are restricted to a few islands off the coast of New Zealand.

◀ The collared lizard has distinctive markings on the back of its head, giving it its name. The long hind legs allow it to run away quickly from predators.

Amazing facts

- The Papuan monitor lizard can grow to 16 feet (5 meters). Its tail makes up most of its length.
- The Gila monster is a poisonous lizard with eight venom glands in its lower jaws. It produces enough venom to kill two adult human beings.
- A Burmese python kept in a safari park in Illinois swallows four or five whole chickens every two weeks.

▲ Snakes have no limbs, but they can move quite rapidly, even when climbing trees.

Squamates

There are three suborders of squamates: snakes, lizards, and worm lizards (amphisbaenians). More than 95 percent of the world's reptiles belong to this order, with lizards forming the largest suborder. Snakes have no limbs or eyelids and are all carnivores. Lizards usually have four limbs, a distinct head, and a long tail. They have adapted to live in a wide range of habitats and are found all over the world. Most lizards are carnivores, although some skinks may eat plants.

Worm lizards are closely related to true lizards. They look like worms, having cylindrical bodies with rings of scales. Most do not have any limbs, and they have adapted to life burrowing underground. They are only found in tropical and subtropical regions.

Crocodilians

Crocodilians are large reptiles with wide, flattened bodies, muscular tails, and long snouts with powerful jaws. Most crocodilians live in or around freshwater lakes, rivers, and lagoons. The saltwater crocodile (*Crocodylus porosus*) is found in both freshwater and marine habitats. All crocodilians are carnivores that lie in wait for their prey with their bodies partly submerged in water.

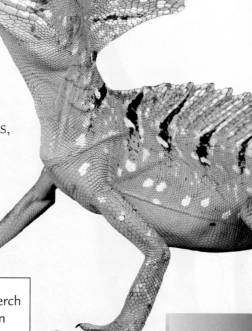

▶ When disturbed, the basilisk drops from its perch in the trees and dives into water to escape. It can run across the surface of still water on its hind legs.

17

Reptiles of the Past

The earliest ancestors of reptiles are believed to have evolved about 300 million years ago. These ancestors became adapted to the hot, dry conditions on land by developing a waterproof skin and producing leathery, shelled eggs that did not need to develop in water. Their skulls were completely covered in bone. Scientists put these vertebrates into a subclass of the reptiles called the Anapsida. They were the first vertebrates to adapt completely to life on land.

Within the Anapsida, two main groups developed. One group gave rise to the ichthyosaurs and plesiosaurs—primitive reptiles that are all extinct. The other group, the chelonians, gave rise to tortoises and turtles. When scientists compared the fossils of ancient turtles with the skeletons of modern turtles, they found very few differences.

Ichthyosaurs and plesiosaurs

The first group of primitive reptiles gave rise to the ichthyosaurs and the plesiosaurs. These two types of reptiles, which scientists placed in the subclass Parapsida, became adapted to marine life. The ichthyosaurs looked like dolphins with flippers and sharklike tails. The plesiosaurs had bodies similar to those of tortoises, with very long necks and paddle-like flippers. There were large numbers of both groups until the end of the Cretaceous Period (65 million years ago), after which they became extinct.

▼ The discovery of fossil bones of large dinosaurs, such as *Tyrannosaurus rex*, has enabled scientists to build models of creatures that lived on Earth millions of years ago.

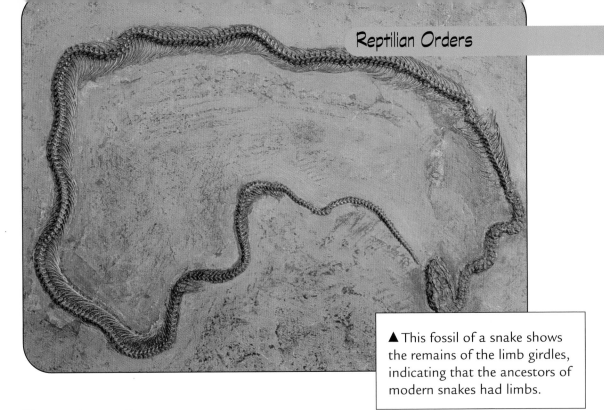

▲ This fossil of a snake shows the remains of the limb girdles, indicating that the ancestors of modern snakes had limbs.

Diapsid reptiles

The diapsid reptiles evolved from the Anapsida. They were divided into two groups: the archosaurs and the lepidosaurs. The archosaurs included the dinosaurs and the pterosaurs. These amazing reptiles roamed Earth for more than 200 million years before becoming extinct about 65 million years ago. The only surviving archosaurs are crocodilians. The lepidosaurs gave rise to snakes, lizards, and tuataras.

Amazing facts

- Many dinosaurs could stand upright on two legs and run fast to escape their enemies or chase their prey.

- The evolution of reptiles occurred at the same time as the evolution and spread of insects. The earliest reptiles were small, lizardlike creatures that ate insects.

- The fossilized footprints of Hadrosaur, a duck-billed dinosaur, were found near Salt Lake City, Utah. They measured about 32 inches (80 centimeters) wide and 54 inches (135 centimeters) long.

▲ This turtle fossil skeleton bears a strong resemblance to the skeleton of a modern turtle.

19

Tortoises and Turtles

Tortoises, turtles, and terrapins belong to an ancient order of reptiles known as chelonians. The earliest known chelonian fossils date from 245 million years ago. Tortoises and turtles living today differ very little from those that lived at the same time as the dinosaurs.

▲ Terrapins have limbs modified for swimming. When they are young, terrapins feed on freshwater invertebrates, such as insects and their larvae.

Classification key

CLASS	Reptilia
ORDER	**Chelonia**
FAMILIES	11
SPECIES	293

Shell

The main features of tortoises and turtles are that they have a shell surrounding the body, four limbs, and a horny, toothless beak. The upper part of the shell is called the carapace, and the lower part is called the plastron. The head and the front legs stick out through openings at the front, and the hind legs and short tail from an opening at the back. Although it is hard and thick, the shell is sensitive because it has nerves embedded in it.

▼ Tortoises and turtles do not have teeth and so cannot chew their food. They use their sharp jaws to snip off pieces of food, which they swallow.

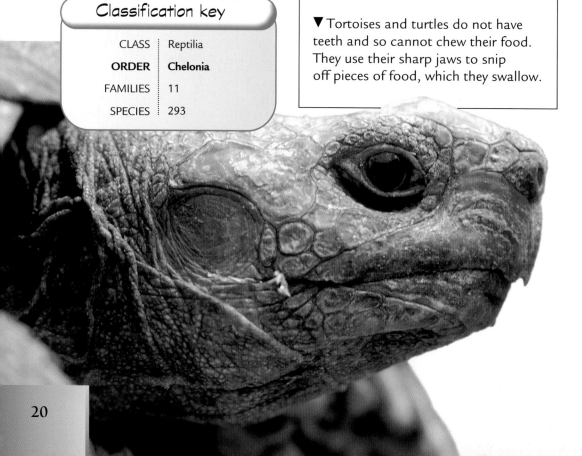

- Tortoises and turtles can live for a long time. A tortoise presented to the Tongan royal family in the 1770s by Captain James Cook lived for more than 188 years until it died in 1965.

- Giant tortoises were once kept on board sailing ships to provide fresh meat during long Pacific sea voyages.

- The number of rings on the scales of a young tortoise or turtle can give some idea of its age. In temperate regions, where there are seasons with variations in the climate, a new ring is added to each scale every year.

▼ Turtles feed on a variety of marine life. Most are herbivores, or plant eaters, although some, like the loggerhead turtle, have jaws strong enough to crush crabs and lobsters.

Chelonians are divided into two groups. In one group, the straight-necked tortoises and turtles, the head is pulled in vertically as the neck bones curve into a *U*-shape. The skin of the neck is tucked in and the opening of the shell is completely blocked by the front legs. The members of the other group, the side-necked tortoises and turtles, have longer necks that are tucked sideways into the openings of the shells. In this group, the front legs are not drawn under the shell.

Some species have hinges on either the carapace or the plastron. In the box turtles, such as the Carolina box turtle, the front section of the plastron is hinged. When the turtle withdraws its head inside the shell, it can raise the hinge to close the hole completely. The serrated hinge-back tortoise boxes itself in with a hinge at the back of the carapace.

Tortoise facts

- Tortoises in deserts escape from the heat by burrowing and becoming torpid, or inactive.
- The American desert tortoise stores water in its enlarged bladder.
- Most desert tortoises get all their moisture from plant food.

▼ These giant tortoises are herbivores. Tortoises with dome-shaped shells feed on grass, while those with saddle-backed shells can stretch their necks further to reach the leaves on bushes and shrubs.

Habitats and habits

Tortoises, turtles, and terrapins are found in tropical regions of the world. However, some species are present in temperate climates. Tortoises are terrestrial, which means they live on land. Terrapins have adapted to live in freshwater and turtles are marine, which means they live in salt water. Many scientists use the word *turtles* to mean all the chelonians and do not distinguish between tortoises, turtles, and terrapins.

Tortoises eat mainly leaves and fruits of plants, although they do eat small animals and animal remains. When they are young, terrapins feed on insect larvae and small aquatic animals. They begin eating aquatic plants as they get older. The diet of turtles is more varied. Some species feed only on seaweed, while others catch jellyfish, mollusks, and sea urchins. Carnivorous species lie in wait for their prey.

▲ The largest freshwater turtle, the alligator snapping turtle, has a small, pink, wormlike structure in its mouth. This is used to entice prey into its mouth. Once the victim, usually a fish, is inside, the jaws are snapped shut quickly.

All tortoises and turtles lay their eggs on land. Once the eggs have been laid, the parents are not involved in caring for the eggs or the young. Tropical species may produce more than one clutch of eggs each year, but in temperate climates, the females usually lay only one clutch.

The giants

The Galapagos tortoises are the largest tortoises in the world. The ancestors of these giants probably floated to the islands from South America on driftwood rafts. They can survive without food and water for months. The giant tortoises may be as long as 5 feet (152 centimeters) and weigh up to 550 pounds (250 kilograms). There is some variation in shell shape and size among these tortoises, depending on which island they come from. These differences have resulted in several subspecies. They have survived and evolved on the Galapagos Islands because they lack competition from other species and also lack predators.

Turtles

Turtles are more streamlined than the terrestrial tortoises. The carapace is flatter, and the limbs are modified for swimming. Smooth, flattened carapaces enable turtles to move easily through the water. The largest species is the leatherback turtle, which can be up to 6 feet (1.8 meters) long. The leatherback is found in many tropical, subtropical, and temperate seas and oceans. These turtles have narrow, leathery shells, large heads, and limbs modified to form flippers for swimming. They may travel great distances to find their food. During the breeding season, females migrate from their feeding grounds back to particular beaches to lay their eggs. The males come ashore to mate with the females.

▶ The shape of this type of shell protects the tortoise from predators.

The Green Turtle

Most green turtles live in shallow, tropical waters. The adults are herbivorous, feeding on eel grass, but young turtles may also eat fish, mollusks, and crustaceans. Two subspecies are known—one in the Pacific Ocean and the other in the Atlantic Ocean.

Migration

Female turtles migrate thousands of miles to return to their breeding sites. Atlantic green turtles, which breed on Ascension Island, feed off the coast of Brazil about 900 miles (1,500 kilometers) away. The adult females visit the island to lay their eggs on the sandy beaches. They then return to their feeding grounds, where they may stay for several years. They always return to the same beach to lay another clutch of eggs. In the tropics, eggs may be laid all year. In other areas, breeding occurs during the hottest months of the year.

▲ Female sea turtles lay eggs in clutches on sandy beaches. They cover the eggs with sand and then leave them.

Classification key

CLASS	Reptilia
ORDER	Testudinae
FAMILY	Cheloniidae
GENUS	Chelonia
SPECIES	***Chelonia mydas***
SUBSPECIES	2 – *Chelonia mydas mydas* (Atlantic green turtle) and *Chelonia mydas agassizii* (Pacific green turtle)

▶ The green turtle is a very efficient swimmer, with a smooth, streamlined shell and powerful flippers. Females migrate long distances to their breeding sites to lay their eggs.

◄Young turtles hatch from their shells by breaking them with special egg teeth. As soon as they hatch, they make their way to the sea.

Nesting and hatching

Females come ashore only to lay their eggs. They drag themselves up the beach to a suitable nesting site above the tide level. Each female digs a hole in the sand with her hind flippers. She then lays about 100 to 150 eggs in the hole. The female covers the eggs with sand, flattening the surface with her flippers. She then returns to the sea, paying no further attention to her eggs.

The incubation of the eggs takes roughly 60 days. In warmer climates, the incubation period is shorter than it is in colder climates. Not all of the eggs will hatch because many are eaten by predators, such as rats, dogs, and people. The young turtles break out of their eggs with the help of the horny egg tooth on the tip of the upper jaw. All the eggs hatch more or less at the same time, so the young turtles emerge in large groups.

Dangerous journey

The young turtles make their way directly to the sea as fast as they can. They do not swim far out to sea, but stay for a while in the shallow waters. On this journey to the water, they may be eaten by crabs and seabirds. Once the hatchlings reach the water, they feed mainly on small invertebrates, such as jellyfish, mollusks, and sponges, that live close to the shore.

Amazing facts

- The green turtle gets its name from the color of its fat.
- A single female green turtle can lay up to 400 eggs in one breeding season.
- Green turtles were once hunted for their meat and eggs. This is now illegal.

Tuataras

Tuataras are the most primitive of all living reptiles. They are the only living relatives of a group of ancient reptiles known as beak head reptiles, which lived more than 200 million years ago. Adult tuataras are brownish-olive in color, with a small, yellow spot in the center of each scale. They can reach 20 to 32 inches (50 to 80 centimeters) long.

Island dwellers

Tuataras are found on about 30 small islands off the coast of New Zealand. During the last century, they became extinct on the mainland because they were hunted by rats, wild cats, and pigs that had been introduced from Europe.

◀ Tuataras live underground. They hunt for their food around the entrances to their burrows.

▼ Tuataras have large heads, but no visible ears. There is a third eye beneath the skin on the top of the head.

Classification key

CLASS	Reptilia
SUBCLASS	**Rhynchocephalia**
SUPERORDER	Sphenodontidae
FAMILY	1
GENUS	*Sphenodon*
SPECIES	2—*punctatus* and *guntheri*

Amazing facts

- Until 1989, *Sphenodon punctatus* was believed to be the only surviving species of tuatara. Studies of the genes of different groups of tuataras have shown that there is a second species, *Sphenodon guntheri*. This second species is found only on one tiny island.

- It takes four times longer for tuatara eggs to hatch than it does for other reptiles.

- Adult tuataras may live for more than 100 years.

▼ Tuataras are usually nocturnal but may be seen basking on rocks during the day. The characteristic crest, which extends down the back and along the tail, is made up of large scales.

Underground burrows

Tuataras live underground in burrows. They can make their own, but more often they live in the burrows of seabirds that inhabit the same areas of seashore. Tuataras stay underground during the day and come out at night to feed on insects, earthworms, and snails. Sometimes they eat the eggs or young of other lizards and birds.

Tuataras are more active at lower temperatures than most other reptiles, with an average body temperature of 42 to 55 °F (6 to 13° C), which is usually lower than their surroundings. Their low temperatures mean that they grow slowly. Female tuataras are not ready to breed until they are about twenty years old.

The females lay about ten to fifteen white eggs with hard shells in shallow holes in the sand, where they are warmed by the sunlight. Parents do not look after the eggs. The young tuataras hatch about fourteen months after the eggs are laid. The females may lay eggs only every three or four years.

Snakes

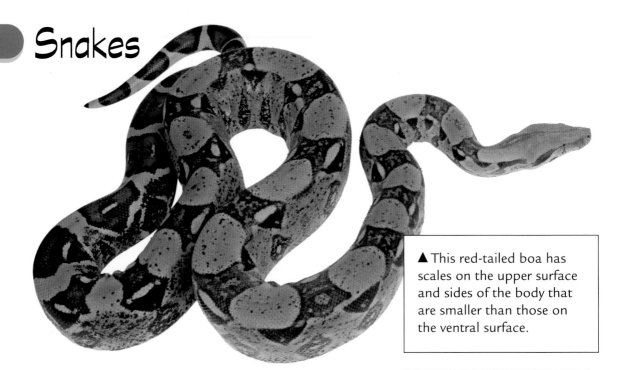

▲ This red-tailed boa has scales on the upper surface and sides of the body that are smaller than those on the ventral surface.

Snakes may live as far north as the Arctic Circle, but most species live in tropical and subtropical areas. Some tropical snakes estivate, or become dormant, during the hottest months of the year. In regions with cold winters, such as the northeastern United States, the snakes hibernate.

Classification key	
CLASS	Reptilia
ORDER	Squamata
SUBORDER	**Serpentes**
FAMILIES	18
SPECIES	About 2,900

Snake movement

A snake's entire body is covered with horny scales arranged in regular rows that usually overlap. On its underside is a single row of wider scales, called the ventral scales or scutes. Each scute on the ventral surface is associated with a single row of scales on the sides and back, and with a single set of muscles. Many snakes, including the king cobra, use side-to-side movements to get around. Wave-like contractions of the muscles cause the snake's body to push sideways against pebbles and other objects, moving it forward.

▼ Snakes have very flexible jaws and are able to swallow large prey. The prey is either suffocated or poisoned first, so that it does not struggle while it is being swallowed.

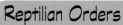
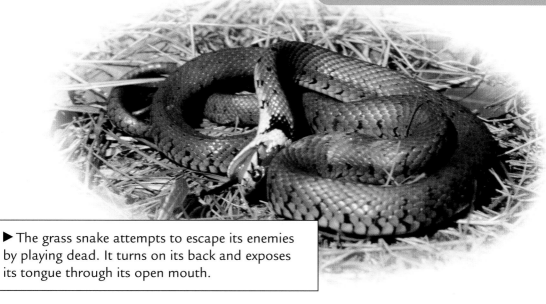

▶ The grass snake attempts to escape its enemies by playing dead. It turns on its back and exposes its tongue through its open mouth.

Heavier snakes, such as the rainbow boa, use enlarged ventral scutes to grip the ground, moving forward like caterpillars. When crossing smooth surfaces and moving in narrow burrows, climbing snakes pull themselves forward by bunching and extending their muscles like a spring, pushing against the walls of the burrow. Desert snakes move by sidewinding. A loop of the body is lifted clear of the ground as the snake moves sideways across the loose sand.

Carnivores

All snakes are carnivores. They eat a wide variety of prey, including insects, snails, mice, and larger animals. Some snakes feed only on other kinds of snakes. Although most snakes have good eyesight, their sense of hearing is poor. They cannot hear sounds through the air, but they can sense vibrations through the ground. Some species have heat receptors that help them track and catch their warm-blooded prey.

Snakes such as cobras and coral snakes produce a poison, called venom, to kill their prey. The venom is produced in special glands and gets into the victims through special teeth, called fangs, when the snake bites its prey. Other snakes, such as boas and pythons, squeeze their prey to death.

Amazing facts

- Most female snakes abandon their eggs as soon as they have laid them. If they bear live young, these are also abandoned.
- The shortest snake is the thread snake, at about 4 inches (11 centimeters) long.
- The longest and heaviest snakes are the anacondas. They have been known to grow to a length of more than 36 feet (11 meters) and weigh more than 880 pounds (400 kilograms).

Boas and Pythons

Boas and pythons include many of the largest, most powerful snakes. They have many primitive features not seen in other groups of snakes. In the skeleton, there are hind limb (pelvic) girdle bones, and some species have a pair of claws or spurs representing all that is left of the hind limbs of their ancestors. All species have two lungs, large, powerful teeth and short, thick tails that can be used to grip tree branches. Tails that can grip things are described as prehensile.

Boas are found in mainly North, Central, and South America, with a few species in Africa, Asia, and the Pacific islands. Pythons are more common in the tropical and subtropical regions of Australia, Africa, Asia, and the Pacific islands.

▼ Emerald tree boas have strong, prehensile tails and are adapted to living in trees. The color of the body blends in with the leaves of the rain forest habitat, concealing the boa from its enemies. It coils itself around a branch and waits, head down, ready to strike its prey.

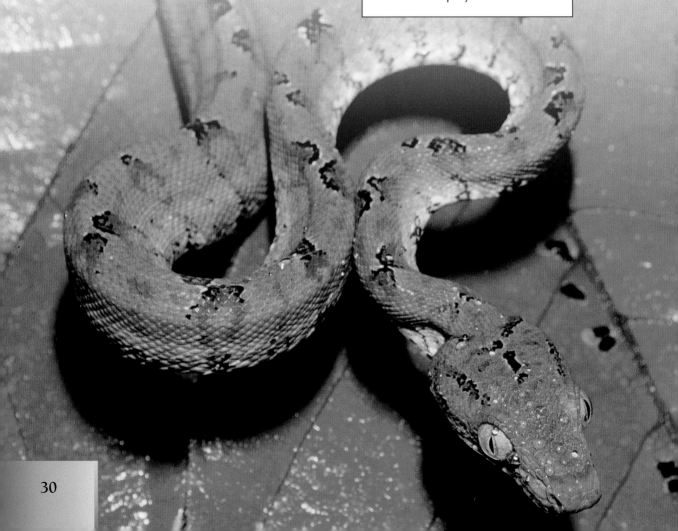

▲ The green tree python is well adapted to living in trees. Its green color provides camouflage in the tree canopy.

Classification key

CLASS	Reptilia
ORDER	Squamata
SUBORDER	Serpentes
SUPERFAMILY	**Caenophidia**
FAMILIES	2—Boidae (boas) and Pythonidae (pythons)
SPECIES	53

Amazing facts

- An African rock python, at about 13 feet (4 meters) long, was once seen swallowing a 130-pound (60-kilogram) impala!

- The common anaconda is the longest snake in the western hemisphere and the heaviest snake in the world. An adult may reach 20 feet (6 meters) in length and weigh 235 pounds (107 kilograms).

- The ball, or royal, python of Africa defends itself by curling up into a ball that can be rolled along the ground.

Death by squeezing

Boas and pythons are nonpoisonous snakes that kill their prey by squeezing, or constricting, it to death and then swallowing it whole. Victims die of suffocation because they cannot breathe and the heart cannot pump blood around the body. This is useful for warm-blooded prey such as mammals and birds because they need to breathe more often. Some constrictors can kill large animals such as deer, wild pigs, and goats.

Live young

Boas give birth to live young. There may be up to 40 young at a time, but they are not cared for by the parents and leave the female immediately after they are born. Pythons lay eggs that are cared for by the female until they hatch. The larger pythons may have clutches of up to 100 eggs. The female coils around the eggs, protecting them from predators and providing an even temperature for their development. Some pythons, such as the Indian and green tree pythons, keep their eggs warm by shivering to generate heat.

▼ The python seizes prey in its jaws and coils its body around the victim. Each time the victim breathes out, the snake tightens its grip.

31

Colubrids

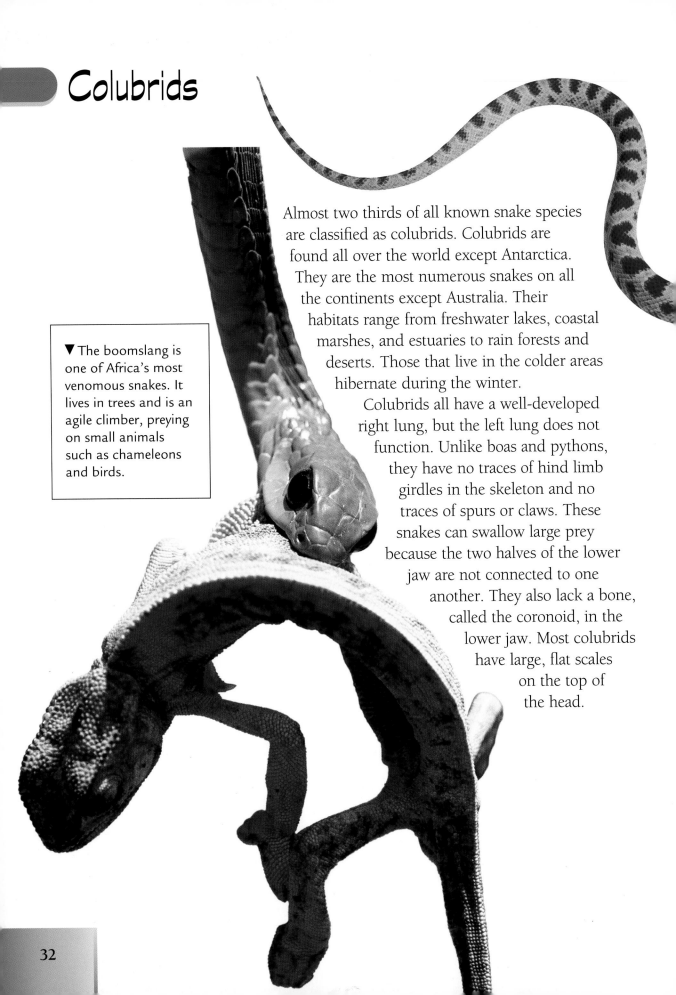

Almost two thirds of all known snake species are classified as colubrids. Colubrids are found all over the world except Antarctica. They are the most numerous snakes on all the continents except Australia. Their habitats range from freshwater lakes, coastal marshes, and estuaries to rain forests and deserts. Those that live in the colder areas hibernate during the winter.

Colubrids all have a well-developed right lung, but the left lung does not function. Unlike boas and pythons, they have no traces of hind limb girdles in the skeleton and no traces of spurs or claws. These snakes can swallow large prey because the two halves of the lower jaw are not connected to one another. They also lack a bone, called the coronoid, in the lower jaw. Most colubrids have large, flat scales on the top of the head.

▼ The boomslang is one of Africa's most venomous snakes. It lives in trees and is an agile climber, preying on small animals such as chameleons and birds.

▼ Corn snakes are found in the southern United States. They use constriction to kill their prey of small rodents, birds, and lizards.

Classification key

CLASS	Reptilia
ORDER	Squamata
SUBORDER	Serpentes
SUPERFAMILY	Caenophidia
FAMILY	**Colubridae**
SPECIES	about 1,600

Poisonous snakes

Most colubrids kill their prey by constriction and are nonvenomous. The venomous species, such as the boomslang, produce venom in a special organ called Duvernoy's gland. In the venomous snakes, the fangs are towards the back of the mouth. Usually, colubrids have only one pair of fangs, but some species have two or three pairs. Each fang is solid, with a groove down the outside. When the snake bites its prey, the venom is released and enters the victim through this groove.

Many colubrids lay eggs, hiding them underground, in rotting vegetation, or hollow parts of trees. Some species, notably the grass snake, share nest sites, which can contain up to 200 eggs. Some colubrids give birth to live young.

Amazing facts

- The egg-eating snakes of Africa feed on birds' eggs during the bird breeding season and then fast for the rest of the year. The eggs are swallowed whole.
- When a boomslang is threatened or alarmed, it puffs up its throat to show the brightly colored skin between the scales.

▼ Garter snakes are common in the United States, Canada, and Mexico. They are nonvenomous, live close to water, and feed on earthworms, frogs, toads, and small fish.

Elapids

▲ Sea kraits hunt for their food in the water, but go ashore to digest food, mate, shed their skin and lay their eggs.

Classification key

CLASS	Reptilia
ORDER	Squamata
SUBORDER	Serpentes
SUPERFAMILY	Caenophidia
FAMILY	**Elapidae**
SPECIES	270

Elapids are among the most poisonous animals in the world. They have slender, cylindrical bodies with smooth, shiny scales. Elapids are found in a wide range of habitats in tropical areas and in the southern hemisphere. Terrestrial species live on the ground, arboreal species live in trees, and aquatic species live in water.

Deadly fangs

Elapids share some features with colubrids because they belong to the same superfamily. One major difference between the two families is that the fangs of elapids are at the front of the mouth and those of most colubrids are at the back. Elapids have grooves on their fangs, and this allows the venom to get into the bite wound. Because the fangs are at the front, venom reaches the wound more quickly and has a greater effect on the victim. The venom of elapids is also more toxic, or poisonous, than that of colubrids. In most elapids, the venom affects the nervous system and paralyzes the muscles that control breathing and the pumping of the heart. The venom may also contain substances that affect the clotting of the blood.

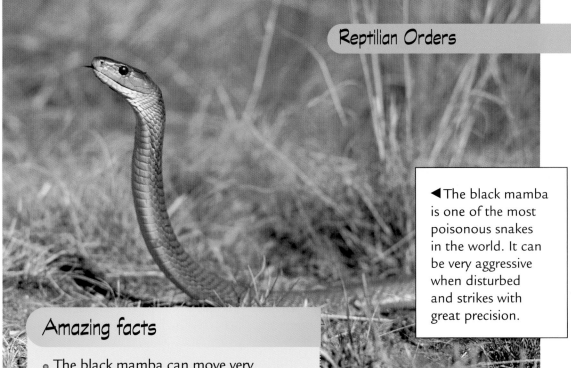

◄ The black mamba is one of the most poisonous snakes in the world. It can be very aggressive when disturbed and strikes with great precision.

Amazing facts

- The black mamba can move very quickly, reaching speeds of about 12 miles (20 kilometers) per hour. This is fast enough to overtake a human being running briskly.

- Most sea snakes can produce about 0.004 to 0.005 ounces (10 to 15 milligrams) of venom. It takes 0.00005 ounces (1.5 milligrams) to kill a person.

- In tiger snakes, mating can last up to seven hours. The female sometimes drags the male around with her.

Camouflage and protection

Many terrestrial elapids are camouflaged so that they blend in with their surroundings. However, others are brightly colored as a warning to predators to keep away. Cobras scare off their enemies by raising the front third of their body and spreading their ribs to form a hood.

Marine snakes

Sea snakes and sea kraits are marine elapids that are found mostly in the seas around Southeast Asia and Australia. They have flattened tails that are adapted for swimming. They feed on fish—mostly eels. Sea snakes are fully aquatic and do not leave the water. They give birth to live young.

▼ When threatened, a coral snake will curl its tail into a spiral and hold it upright. This attracts predators away from the head.

The Cobra

▲ The spitting, or black-necked, cobra from Africa can spray a mixture of venom and saliva at the eyes of its prey, causing temporary blindness.

Cobra is the common name for a group of poisonous elapids that, when disturbed, raise the front part of their bodies from the ground and spread their hoods. This display is meant to frighten their enemies. The hood is formed by spreading out the ribs in the upper part of the body behind the head. Cobras are found mainly in southern Asia, Africa, and the Philippines. They feed mainly on small mammals, birds, lizards, and other snakes.

King cobra

The king cobra lives in the forests of Southeast Asia and hunts other snakes. It has a long body with smooth scales and can swim well. Male and female cobras pair off and stay together during the breeding season. After mating, the females lay between 20 and 40 eggs in piles of loose, dead leaves. Both parents are involved in guarding the eggs until they hatch. Then the young go off and fend for themselves.

Classification key

CLASS	Reptilia
ORDER	Squamata
SUBORDER	Serpentes
SUPERFAMILY	Caenophidia
FAMILY	Elapidae
GENERA	*Naja* and *Ophiophagus*
SPECIES	4—*Ophiophagus Hannah* (king cobra), *Naja naja* (Indian cobra), *Naja haje* (Egyptian cobra), *Naja nigricollis* (black-necked cobra)

Indian and Egyptian cobras

Both the Indian cobra and the Egyptian cobra are found near human settlements. The Indian cobra is found near paddy fields and roadside mud banks, and the Egyptian cobra lives in urban areas and cultivated fields as well as grassland areas. These cobras can kill human beings with their bite unless the antivenin (cure) is given very quickly.

▲ When threatened, a cape cobra can raise the front part of its body off the ground. The head may strike downward, but the snake rarely tries to bite from this position.

Amazing facts

- Snake charmers use cobras in their displays, playing music to entice a snake out of its basket. The cobras cannot really hear the music. However, they rise up anyway and spread their hoods when they are disturbed.

- Ancient Egyptians worshiped the Egyptian cobra and used it as a symbol on pharaohs' crowns.

◀ The main predator of the cobra is the mongoose. A mongoose will launch a series of attacks on a cobra to make it strike out. As the cobra begins to tire, the mongoose tries to deliver a fatal bite to the back of the snake's head.

Vipers

Vipers are found in most temperate and tropical regions of the world except Australia. Some species live in deserts and others in rain forests. However, some vipers are found in Arctic regions.

Dangerous snakes

Vipers are venomous snakes that have a pair of long, hollow fangs in the front of the upper jaw. The venom is produced by large glands in the head and stored in a venom sac. The fangs fold back against the upper part of the mouth when not in use and swing forward into position when the snake is about to strike. When the snake bites, it squeezes the venom sac. This pushes venom into the fangs, which act like hypodermic syringes that force venom into the victim. These snakes strike rapidly, withdraw their fangs, and wait for the victim to die.

Amazing facts

- Although the venom of a bushmaster is not very poisonous in small doses, the snake's long fangs produce a deep bite that inject large volumes of venom into the victim.

- The cottonmouth, or water moccasin, lives in the swamps of the southeastern United States. When threatened, it holds its mouth open, exposing a white lining.

▼ Vipers are the most highly evolved of all snakes. They have long, hinged fangs. When threatened and ready to strike its attacker, a bush viper draws its head back to form an *S*-shaped coil with its neck.

▲ Rattlesnakes are recognized by the horny rattle at the end of the tail. When disturbed, the snake vigorously shakes the rattle to scare predators. The rattle is made up of cone-shaped sections of skin that remain after the snake molts. A new section is added each time the skin is shed.

True vipers and pit vipers

Vipers are divided into two groups: the true vipers, which include adders, and the pit vipers, which include the rattlesnake, copperhead, and cottonmouth. Pit vipers have deep pits on each side of the head between the eye and the nostril. These pits contain heat sensitive cells that allow the snake to detect warm-blooded prey in the dark.

Vipers have short, thick bodies and often have prehensile tails. The head is triangular and quite distinct from the neck. Vipers do not move very quickly. They depend on their coloring to hide from their prey and predators. Many vipers have intricate patterns and markings on their skin. This helps to break up their outline and contribute to their camouflage. Some vipers lay eggs, but most give birth to live young. Many species breed every two or three years. During the nonbreeding years, vipers feed and build up their body weight.

Classification key

CLASS	Reptilia
ORDER	Squamata
SUBORDER	Serpentes
SUPERFAMILY	Caenophidia
FAMILY	**Viperidae**
SPECIES	228

▼ The European adder is venomous, but it is less aggressive than most venomous snakes. Bites to human beings are rarely fatal. The adder is most widely distributed snake in the viper family.

Lizards

Lizards are the largest group of reptiles. Most lizards are small with four legs and a long tail. They range in size from the smallest geckos, about 0.8 inches (2 centimeters long), to monitor lizards, which can grow to 10 feet (3 meters long). Lizards live all over the world except Antarctica. They are most common in the tropical and subtropical regions, but a few species are found in cooler, temperate climates. Most lizards live on the ground, but others live in trees or in underground burrows. Some lizards are partly aquatic.

Classification key

CLASS	Reptilia
ORDER	Squamata
SUBORDER	**Lacertilia**
SUPERFAMILIES	4 – Iguania (Iguanas and chameleons), Gekkota (Geckos), Scincomorpha (Skinks), Anguimorpha (Monitors)
FAMILIES	19
SPECIES	about 4500

◀ A lizard's limbs are held at right angles to the body. Each limb has five digits. When a lizard walks, its tail swings from side to side, balancing the body's movements .

Amazing facts

- There are only two venomous lizards: the Mexican beaded lizard and the Gila monster.
- When threatened, the horned lizard sprays an intruder with blood from the corners of its eyes.
- The basilisk can walk upright on its hind legs and can run on water.

Walking on all fours

Most lizards walk on all fours. Those that live in trees have sharp claws that give them a good grip. Some lizards that burrow underground have well-developed front limbs for digging. Other underground species may have reduced limbs. The flying lizard can glide using winglike pieces of skin stretched between its elongated ribs. If the lizard needs to move from tree to tree, it moves its ribs outward and opens the flaps of skin.

Most lizards prey on insects and other small creatures. However, some, such as the green iguana, eat plants. The Gila monster, which lives in desert areas, eats small rodents and the eggs of other reptiles and birds. Most lizards have sharp teeth and good eyesight to help them find prey easily.

▲ Most lizards have a long tail that can be shed if they are attacked. A replacement tail grows, but in the new part the arrangement of the scales and the color may be slightly different.

Defense

If caught by the tail, some lizards escape by shedding the tail. This defense mechanism, known as autotomy, is very effective because the detached tail may twitch for some time after it has broken off. The lizard is able to grow a new tail, but it is not always exactly the same color as the original one. A lizard may break its tail more than once during its life. Other defense mechanisms include camouflage, changing of color, or threat displays.

▶ Some lizards, such as this leaf chameleon, have adapted to climbing trees. The prehensile tail and toes help the chameleon grip the branches easily.

41

Chameleons and Iguanas

Iguania is a superfamily of colorful lizards found in a wide range of habitats, including deserts, grassland, and rain forests. There are three families: the iguanas are found in North, Central, and South America; the agamids live mostly in Africa, Asia, and Australia; and the chameleons are found in Africa, Asia, and Europe.

Color changes

The agamids and the iguanas look alike and live in similar types of habitats. However, iguanas can replace lost teeth, but agamids cannot. All the species are able to change their color. However, the chameleons are able to change their color more quickly than either of the other two groups can.

Amazing facts

- A thorny devil can eat up to 3,000 ants in a single meal, at a rate of 45 per minute.
- Basilisks are harmless, but they look very fierce. They are named after a mythical monster that killed its victims by looking at or breathing on them.
- Marine iguanas get rid of salt they do not need through special nasal glands. The salt stays as a crust on the skin and makes them look white.

▼ Chameleons are tree dwellers adapted to catching insects. The chameleon stalks its prey and then shoots out its long, sticky tongue to catch its victim.

The thorny devil feeds on ants. It has adapted to life in Australian deserts by being able to use all the water that falls on its skin. The water runs into tiny grooves and collects by the corners of the mouth.

Chameleons have cells in their skins that contain colored substances, or pigments. These special cells are called chromatophores. When these cells grow, the skin becomes darker, and when the cells shrink, the skin becomes paler. The pigment cells are affected by chemicals in the blood called hormones.

A chameleon may change its color because it is threatened by an enemy, to communicate with other chameleons, or to control its body temperature. They can also change color in the presence of a member of the opposite sex. Chameleons do not change color to match their backgrounds. If they become frightened or angry, they become darker. During the early part of the day, a chameleon becomes darker so that it absorbs more heat and warms up. At night, chameleons become paler.

Iguanas and agamids change color to communicate with members of the opposite sex during the breeding season.

Classification key

CLASS	Reptilia
ORDER	Squamata
SUBORDER	Lacertilia
SUPERFAMILY	**Iguania**
FAMILIES	3 (Iguanas, agamids and chameleons)
SPECIES	1,412

▶ Iguanas are found in North and South America, Madagascar, and on some Pacific islands.

43

Geckos and Skinks

Geckos get their name from the clicking noise that they make. They are the only lizards that can make sounds. They use the sounds to defend their territory and to attract mates. Geckos are slender with thick, stumpy tails, large, fat heads, and large eyes. Their skin is often coated with tiny, beadlike scales. The eyes of most geckos are covered by a transparent membrane that they lick clean with the tongue. Most geckos are nocturnal. Their skins are usually grey or brown so that they cannot be seen easily by predators in the dark. Geckos that are diurnal, or active during the day, are often brightly colored.

Some geckos live on the ground, but many are tree dwellers. Most climbing geckos have thousands of fine, hairlike structures on the underside of their toes. The tips of the toes are often rounded and large. Most ground-dwelling geckos have claws on their toes.

▼ Geckos have five toes on each limb. Expanded toe pads spread out to help with climbing.

▲ Skinks search for food during the day and take shelter under logs or stones at night.

Skinks

Skinks and their relatives form a superfamily of mostly ground-dwelling lizards. They have long, slender bodies and tails and wedge-shaped heads. Skinks are found all over the world, but are most common in tropical and subtropical regions. Most are found among leaf litter on the ground, but some species live in trees and others burrow underground. The burrowers have small legs or no legs at all. Most skinks will lose their tails if attacked.

Some skink species lay eggs, but others give birth to live young. In some of the egg-laying species, the females stay with the eggs to keep them warm during development. Some relatives of skinks, whiptails, and wall lizards can reproduce without males in a process known as parthenogenesis. The females lay fertile eggs that hatch into exact replicas of the females.

Classification key

CLASS	Reptilia
ORDER	Squamata
SUBORDER	Lacertilia
SUPERFAMILIES	**Gekkota (geckos) and Scincomorpha (skinks)**
SPECIES	Gekkota—1054 and Scincomorpha—1890

Amazing facts

● Many geckos store food in their tails. When food is plentiful, the tail becomes fatter. If food is scarce, the stores are used and the tail becomes thinner.

● The armadillo skink has a body covered with sharp spines. When threatened, it curls into a ball with its tail in its mouth to frighten its enemies and protect itself.

● Some geckos are cannibals. For example, the tokay eats other tokays as well as insects and small invertebrates.

◄ The tokay gecko is nocturnal. During the day, the pupils of its eyes are reduced to vertical slits with three tiny holes.

Monitors

Monitor lizards are large, heavy lizards that belong to the family Varanidae. They live in tropical and desert areas of Africa, Asia, the East Indies, and Australia.

Monitor lizards have long, heavy bodies with elongated heads and necks. Their legs are short and sturdy, and they have powerful tails. All monitor lizards have long, forked tongues that they flick in and out. Different species range in size from about 8 inches to 10 feet (20 centimeters to 3 meters) long. Depending on their size, monitor lizards feed on insects, small mammals, birds, reptiles, and their eggs. Some will feed on carrion, the dead remains of other animals.

Most monitors live on the ground. However, some, such as the green tree monitor, can climb trees. The Nile monitor is found in and around water. It feeds on fish and frogs as well as birds and their eggs. The largest monitor is the Komodo dragon, which is found in Indonesia. This fierce lizard is a predator and a scavenger.

Classification key

CLASS	Reptilia
ORDER	Squamata
SUBORDER	Protocanthopterygii
SUPERFAMILY	**Anguimorpha**
FAMILIES	6 (including the monitors, slow worms, glass lizards, Gila monster)
SPECIES	173

▲ Monitors, such as this desert monitor, have long necks, narrow heads, and pointed snouts. Their long, forked tongues are used to gain information about their surroundings.

- A Gila monster's tail is short and blunt. It stores fat that the lizard can live on for months.
- Many monitors incubate their eggs in termite nests. The females break open the nests, lay their eggs, and let the termites seal up the damaged parts of the nest.

▶ The Gila monster eats small rodents and the eggs of other reptiles.

Anguids

Closely related to the monitors are the anguids, a group of lizards with smooth scales and long, slender bodies. These lizards have either very small legs or no legs at all. The slow worm, which is found in Europe as well as parts of Asia and Africa, is often mistaken for a snake. However, it has movable eyelids and can shed its brittle tail easily. The tail is quite slow to regrow, so the adults can look quite stumpy.

Glass lizards, sometimes called glass snakes, are also anguids and are related to the slow worms. They get their name from the smooth, hard, shiny scales on their bodies. Glass lizards have extremely long tails that they shed when threatened.

Poisonous lizards

There are only two poisonous lizards: the Gila monster and its close relative, the Mexican beaded lizard. In both lizards, the venom glands are in the lower jaw. The lizards bite into their victims, holding onto them while the venom gets into the wounds made by their teeth.

◀ The sand monitor, also known as Gould's goanna, is one of the largest monitors in Australia. It feeds on mammals, birds, and other reptiles.

The Komodo Dragon

The Komodo dragon is the world's largest lizard. Adults may reach lengths of 7 to 10 feet (2 to 3 meters). It is found on the islands of Indonesia in lowland areas of open grassland, on hillsides, and in open woodlands.

A Komodo dragon has a small head, a long neck, and a muscular tail usually longer than its body. The limbs are sturdy and hold the body clear off the ground when walking. When a Komodo dragon stands on its hind legs, it can use its tail as a prop. Although these lizards are large, they can move fast over short distances.

Eggs and young

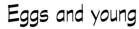

Females lay up to 25 eggs in a nest in sandy ground. The eggs take about 9 months to hatch. There is no parental care at all, and adult Komodo dragons will kill and eat the young. Young Komodo dragons take about five years to mature. During this time they feed on smaller prey, such as snakes, lizards, and rodents. They keep away from the adults to avoid being eaten.

▲ Young Komodo dragons hatch by breaking through the egg shell with their egg teeth. They have to fend for themselves immediately as there is no parental care.

Lizard hunter

The Komodo eats anything it can catch. It hunts and ambushes deer, goats, and wild boars. It is also known to eat carrion. It has good eyesight, a good sense of smell, and is usually active during the day.

Amazing facts

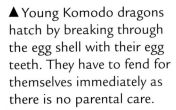

- A Komodo dragon can detect the scent of decaying meat up to 10 feet (3 meters) away.
- Males fight each other for the chance to mate. They stand on their hind legs, using their tails as props, and wrestle.

Classification key

CLASS	Reptilia
ORDER	Squamata
SUBORDER	Lacertilia
SUPERFAMILY	Anguimorpha
FAMILY	Varanidae
GENUS	*Varanus*
SPECIES	***Varanus komodoensis***

◄ Although the jaws are wide with sharp, serrated teeth, the Komodo dragon cannot chew its prey. There are sharp claws on the digits for holding prey and also for digging.

Poisonous saliva

The Komodo dragon seizes prey with its jaws and bites it, but the prey does not die right away. The dragon's saliva contains poisonous bacteria that infect the wound, and this is what kills the prey. The dragon then feeds on the decaying victim. The dragon cannot chew its food. Instead, it bites off pieces and pushes them into the back of its mouth.

◄ The Komodo dragon flicks its long, forked tongue in and out as it searches for carrion or tracks its prey.

49

Crocodiles and Alligators

Crocodiles and alligators belong to the order Crocodilia. They have long bodies with long, flattened tails. Their bodies are covered in horny scales that form a tough protective covering. The scales on the belly are smooth and soft. The tough scales on the back give the reptiles their armor-plated appearance. Their snouts are long, with powerful jaws and strong teeth.

▲ The gharial's long, narrow snout and scissorlike jaws make it easy to recognize. This type of jaw is well adapted for catching fish.

Classification key

CLASS	Reptilia
ORDER	**Crocodilia**
FAMILIES	3 (True crocodiles, alligators and caimans, gharials)
SPECIES	23

Life in water

Most crocodilians live in freshwater, but the largest crocodile, the estuarine or saltwater crocodile, can swim in the sea. All crocodilians are well adapted to life in water. Eyes and ear openings are on the top of the head so that crocodilians can see and even hear when almost totally submerged. When swimming under water, they can close their ears and nostrils with special flaps of skin. The eyes have a transparent covering called the nictitating membrane, which protects the eyes under water. Webbed hind feet enable crocodilians to paddle slowly, but they can use their powerful tails and streamlined bodies for more rapid movement.

▲ Crocodilians are carnivores. They lie in wait at the edges of lakes and rivers for their prey to come within range. Crocodilians cannot chew their food, so they swallow birds, small mammals, and fish whole.

Amazing facts

- The saltwater crocodile is the world's largest reptile, growing to a length of about 20 feet (7 meters) and weighing up to 1 ton.
- Nile crocodiles can reach speeds of 30 miles (45 kilometers) per hour when running on land.
- Female crocodilians can lay between 10 and 90 eggs at a time, depending on the species.

Three families

There are three families of crocodilians. They are separated from each other by the shape of the snout and the arrangement of the teeth. True crocodiles (Crocodylidae), which include the Nile crocodile and the dwarf crocodile, live in the swamps and rivers of Asia, Australia, Central and South America, and Africa. True crocodiles have long snouts. The fourth tooth of each half of the lower jaw fits into a notch on the side of the upper jaw and can be seen when the mouth is closed. Alligators and caimans (Alligatoridae), which are found mainly in North, Central, and South America, have shorter, broader snouts. The fourth tooth cannot be seen when the mouth is closed. The gharials (Gavialidae), found in the large lakes and rivers of India and Burma, have very long snouts, and each jaw has more than 50 teeth. Those at the front are enlarged but the ones behind are all the same size and shape.

▶ Crocodiles swim effortlessly under water, surfacing to snap up their prey.

The Nile Crocodile

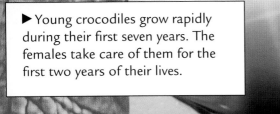

▶ Young crocodiles grow rapidly during their first seven years. The females take care of them for the first two years of their lives.

The Nile crocodile is found along the shores of rivers and lakes and in freshwater swamps in tropical Africa and Madagascar. It got its name because it was first associated with the Nile River. However, it is no longer found in Egypt.

▲ The body temperature of the Nile crocodile can be kept constant by alternately basking in the sun to warm up and moving to the shade or into the water to cool off.

Cooling off

For two to three hours after dawn, Nile crocodiles bask in the sun to replace heat lost from being in the water at night. Usually their jaws are wide open and they lose excess heat through the evaporation of moisture from the mouth. When the sun is overhead, the crocodiles move into the shade or slip back into the water where it is cooler. In the late afternoon, the crocodiles bask for another two or three hours before returning to the water at around dusk. Most of their hunting and feeding is done at night.

Breeding

Male Nile crocodiles are territorial. They live in an area that they guard and defend, fighting off other males that come near. During the mating season, the dominant male in a group drives away rivals.

Two months after mating, the female lays 16 to 80 hard-shelled eggs in a nest she has dug above the water level. The entrance to the nest is closed with sand and grass. Each female stays nearby to protect the eggs from predators. After about 90 days, the young crocodiles make high-pitched chirping noises just before hatching. The female then unblocks the entrance of the nest so that the young can get out. The female carries her young down to the water in her mouth.

The young stay together as a group that is protected by the female, for up to two years. This protection is vital because the young are preyed upon by monitors, turtles, and birds, such as purple herons (*Ardea purpurea*).

During the first 7 years of their lives, Nile crocodiles grow about 12 inches (30 centimeters) a year. The adults can survive on about 5.5 pounds (2.5 kilograms) of food a day. If they eat large prey, they may not feed again for several days. Nile crocodiles are ready to mate when they are about 10 years old.

Amazing facts

- The Nile crocodile is the largest of the four crocodile species found in Africa, with a maximum length of over 10 feet (6 meters). It may reach over 1,540 pounds (700 kilograms) in weight.
- The estimated wild population of Nile crocodiles is only 250,000 to 500,000.
- Nile crocodiles may live for up to 80 years in captivity, but they usually have a life span of 45 years in the wild.

Classification key

CLASS	Reptilia
ORDER	Crocodilia
FAMILY	Crocodylidae
GENUS	*Crocodylus*
SPECIES	***Crocodylus niloticus***

▲ After hatching, the female carries the young down to the water in her mouth.

53

Reptiles Under Threat

According to the International Union for the Conservation of Nature and Natural Resources (IUCN), 55 reptile species are in danger of extinction. They include turtles, some snakes and lizards, and the Chinese alligator. Many more species are considered to be endangered or vulnerable.

Changing habitats

The disappearance of the rain forests and the clearing of natural grasslands for farming have altered reptile habitats. The changes that have occurred on oceanic islands have had the greatest effect on reptiles. Humans have introduced domestic animals, such as dogs, sheep, and cattle, that compete with the reptiles for food or prey upon them or their young. Changes in the use of land also destroy habitats. On some islands, for example, more building has taken place, and marine turtle nesting sites have been disturbed. An increase in tourism can also be a threat to animal species.

▼ Adult turtles can become tangled up in the drift nets used by fishers for catching shrimp.

▲ Snakes are hunted for their skins and sometimes for their meat. Snakeskin shoes are extremely expensive.

Amazing facts

- The Chinese alligator is one of the most endangered of all crocodilian species. Fewer than 150 remain in the wild. They live in 10 ponds in the Anhui Province of the People's Republic of China.

- An Australian skink, the pygmy blue tongue, had not been seen since 1959 and was presumed to be extinct. It was rediscovered in 1992 in small patches of grassland in southern Australia.

Hunting and collecting

Hunting has been a serious threat to many reptile species. Marine turtles are easy to catch when they come to the surface of the water to breathe. They cannot move quickly on land, so they are easily caught by poachers, and their eggs are taken by collectors. They are hunted for their meat and shells. For example, the hawksbill turtle has an attractively marked shell that is used to make combs and trinkets. Lizards, snakes, and crocodilians have been killed for their skins, which are used to make shoes and leather goods. Boas and pythons have been killed for their meat.

Some reptiles are popular as pets. Tortoises, lizards, and some snakes are collected and exported from their native countries. If these animals are not properly cared for, they die.

▼ Crocodilians are hunted for their skins, which are used to make shoes and leather goods. In many countries, it is now illegal to buy or sell reptiles or to export reptile skins.

Protecting Reptiles

The natural habitat of a species should provide all it needs for survival. By setting up national parks and wildlife reserves, many natural habitats are preserved and there is little need for interference from humans if the areas are large enough. In many such areas, steps are taken to prevent poaching and hunting. One of the disadvantages of setting up reserves is that they become popular places for tourism. Turtle hatcheries have become popular places to visit, and care is needed to prevent visitors from disturbing the females as they come ashore to nest.

Wildlife tourism can help conserve species and protect habitats. People will pay to be taken to see animals in their natural habitats. This brings in money to keep the habitat in its natural state and to employ park rangers. It is possible to control the number of tourists so that the animals are disturbed as little as possible.

Breeding programs

One way of preserving species is to breed them in captivity. This can be done in zoos and reserves, attracting tourists at the same time. For some turtles, eggs are collected from nesting sites and put into incubators to keep them warm.

Amazing facts

- The gharial almost became extinct during the 1970s. However, breeding in captivity is helping restore their numbers.
- In Australia, no reptile is known to have become extinct since 1788. In fact, during the last 20 years, 270 species have been discovered and described.

▼ Zoos and nature reserves enable people to see endangered species without disturbing the natural environment too much.

◄ Wildlife tourism is extremely popular. It brings in money to employ park rangers. Wildlife tourism programs can also control the numbers of tourists to protect the environment.

The eggs are protected from illegal collectors and also from predators. After hatching, the young turtles are released so they can make their way to the sea. On the Galapagos Islands, the Charles Darwin Research Station has a breeding program to increase the numbers of giant tortoises. The young animals are released into their natural habitats.

Legislation

Countries can pass laws and make agreements that ban the killing of animals or limit the number that can be killed. However, it can be costly to make sure that the laws are obeyed. An organization called CITES (Convention on International Trade in Endangered Species) was set up to control the trade in wild plants and animals and their products. In countries that belong to this organization, it is now illegal to buy or sell more than 400 species of reptiles, including many turtles. The export of reptile skins, turtle shells, and other products from reptiles is banned in many countries.

◄ Turtle nesting sites are guarded to prevent poachers from stealing and selling the eggs. Sometimes the eggs are collected and kept in special hatcheries. After hatching, the young turtles are released into the wild.

57

Classification

Scientists know of about two million different kinds of animals. With so many species, it is important that they be classified into groups so that they can be described more accurately. The groups show how living organisms are related through evolution and where they belong in the natural world. A scientist identifies an animal by looking at features such as the number of legs or the type of teeth. Animals that share the same characteristics belong to the same species. Scientists place species with similar characteristics in the same genus. The genera are grouped together in families, which in turn are grouped into orders, and orders are grouped into classes. Classes are grouped together in phyla and finally, phyla are grouped into kingdoms. Kingdoms are the largest groups. There are five kingdoms: monerans (bacteria), protists (single-celled organisms), fungi, plants, and animals.

▼ The full name of the saltwater crocodile is *Crocodylus porosus*.

Naming an animal

Each species has a unique Latin name that consists of two words. The first word is the name of the genus to which the organism belongs. The second is the name of its species. For example, the Latin name of the Nile crocodile is *Crocodylus niloticus*. That of the saltwater crocodile is *Crocodylus porosus*. This tells us that these animals are grouped in the same genus but are different species. Many animals are given common names that may vary from one part of the world to another. For example, *Varanus flavirufus*, an anguimorph lizard found in Australia and New Guinea, is known as the sand monitor, Gould's monitor, or Gould's goanna. Sometimes there are very small differences between individuals that belong to the same species. So there is an extra division called a subspecies. To show that an animal belongs to a subspecies, another name is added on to the end of the Latin name. On the island of Isabela (Albermarle Island), there are three giant turtle subspecies: *Geochelone nigra guntheri*, *Geochelone nigra microphyes,* and *Geochelone nigra vicina*.

This table shows how an adder is classified.

Classification	Example: adder	Features
Kingdom	Animalia	Vipers belong to the kingdom Animalia because they have many cells, need to eat food, and are formed from a fertilized egg.
Phylum	Chordata	An animal from the phylum Chordata has a strengthening rod called a notochord down its back and gill pouches at some stage in its life cycle.
Subphylum	Vertebrata	In the subphylum Vertebrata, the notochord is replaced by a backbone made of vertebrae.
Class	Reptilia	Reptiles have tough skin covered with scales, lay eggs with shells, and are ectothermic.
Order	Squamata	Squamates are reptiles with two holes in the temple bones on either side of the skull. This order includes snakes and lizards.
Suborder	Serpentes	Vipers are classified as snakes because they have no legs, no external ears, and are all carnivorous.
Family	Viperidae	The adder is part of this family, which has long, hollow fangs that are folded back when not in use. They all have venom glands, triangular heads, and thick bodies.
Genus	*Vipera*	*Viperus* is the genus for the adder.
Species	*berus*	A species is a group of individuals that can interbreed successfully. The adder's species name is *Vipera berus*.

Reptile Evolution

The origins of reptiles go back millions of years. They evolved from amphibians and were the dominant group of vertebrates for millions of years. The greatest number of different reptile groups evolved during the Mesozoic Era about 230 million years ago. This time is called the Age of Reptiles.

Most of the giant dinosaurs evolved and flourished during the Jurassic and Cretaceous periods about 195 to 65 million years ago. By the end of the Cretaceous period, all these massive reptiles had disappeared. Some scientists believe that the climate changed from warm and humid to cold and dry. This could have altered the plants that were the food of herbivorous dinosaurs. If the herbivores could not find food, they would begin to die out. As a result, the carnivorous dinosaurs would have less food and themselves begin to die out. Only those groups that could adapt to the changing conditions would survive. Modern reptiles are the descendants of certain groups that survived and were able to compete with the emerging mammals and birds.

The most ancient group of reptiles to survive are the chelonians. They have changed very little since they evolved during the Permian period— 280 to 225 million years ago. The tuataras also evolved at this time. The crocodilians are the last surviving group of the ancient archosaurs, so they are the most closely related to the great dinosaurs. The most recent reptile groups to evolve were the squamates and snakes, which are more advanced than the lizards.

▲ Snakes are considered to be the most highly evolved of the reptiles and have adapted to a wide variety of habitats.

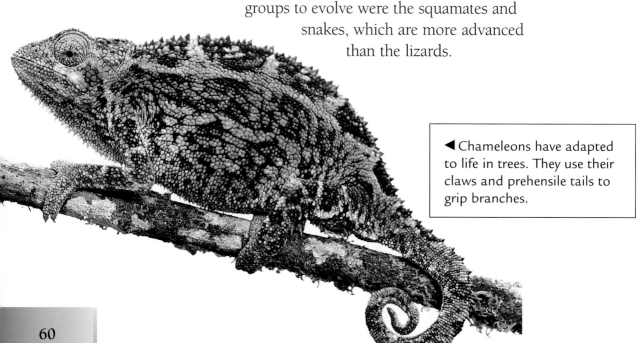

◀ Chameleons have adapted to life in trees. They use their claws and prehensile tails to grip branches.

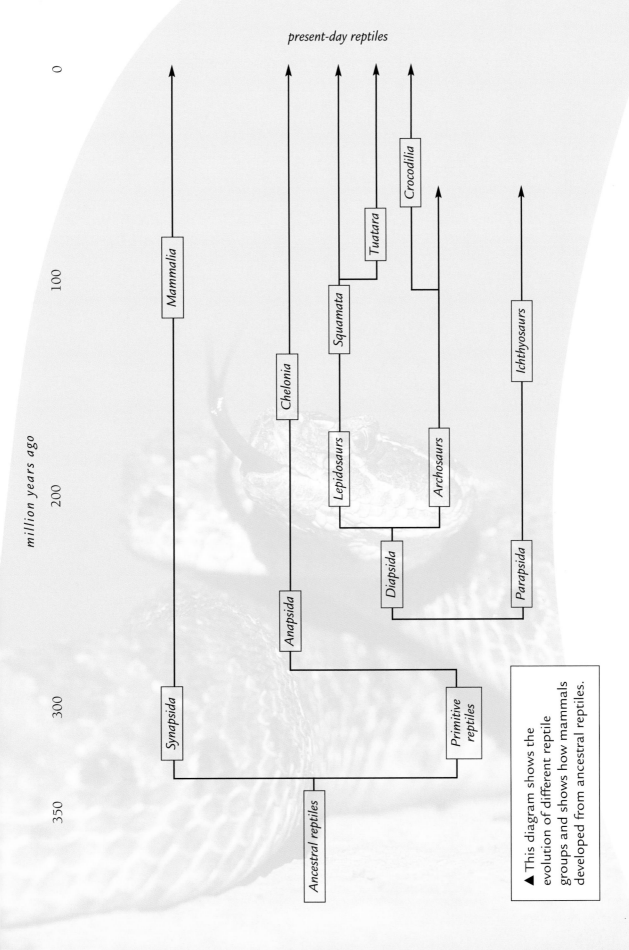

million years ago

0

100

200

300

350

present-day reptiles

Mammalia

Chelonia

Squamata

Tuatara

Crocodilia

Lepidosaurs

Archosaurs

Ichthyosaurs

Synapsida

Anapsida

Diapsida

Parapsida

Primitive reptiles

Ancestral reptiles

▲ This diagram shows the evolution of different reptile groups and shows how mammals developed from ancestral reptiles.

Glossary

adapt change in order to cope with the environment

amphibian animal that lives part of its life on land and part in water, though there are a few exceptions

aquatic living in water

arboreal living in trees

autotomy ability to replace a damaged part of the body, such as a lizard's tail

breed mate and produce young

camouflage coloring that blends with the background, making an animal difficult to see

carapace upper part of the shell in tortoises and turtles

carnivore animal that eats meat

carrion remains of dead animals

characteristic feature or quality of an animal, such as having scales or claws

clutch group of eggs laid at the same time

crustacean arthropod with jointed legs and two pairs of antennae, such as a shrimp or crab

diurnal active during the day

ectothermic having a body temperature that rises and falls with the temperature of the environment

egg tooth hard point on the front of the mouth of a young reptile, used to break through the eggshell during hatching

embryo young animal during its development, before it hatches from the egg or is born

estivation period of dormancy during hot weather

evaporate change in state from a liquid to a gas, such as when water changes from a liquid to a gas

evolution slow process of change in living organisms so that they can adapt to their environment

evolve change very slowly over a long period of time

extinct permanently disappeared

fang special tooth that is either hollow or has grooves, through which venom is injected into the prey's bloodstream

fertilize cause a female to produce young through the introduction of male reproductive material

fossil remains, trace, or impression of ancient life preserved in rock

gland organ that releases a substance such as venom

herbivore animal that eats plants

hibernate fall into a deep winter sleep

incubation period time between egg laying and hatching

incubator place where eggs are kept at the right temperature for their correct development

interbreed mate with another individual of the same species

invertebrate animal without a backbone, such as an insect or jellyfish

Jacobson's organ organ in the roof of the mouth of snakes and lizards that is sensitive to chemical substances in the air

larva (plural: **larvae**) young animal that looks different from the adult and changes shape as it develops

mammal class of vertebrates that feed their young milk, are usually covered in hair, and have a constant body temperature

mate ability of male to fertilize the eggs of a female of the same species

migration regular journey made by an animal, often linked to changes in the seasons

mollusk invertebrate with, most typically, a head, a muscular foot, and an external shell, such as a snail or a clam

molt shedding of the skin in reptiles to allow for growth and to replace worn-out skin

nictitating membrane thin membrane that moves sideways across the eye

nocturnal active at night

organism living being

oviparous animal that lays eggs

ovoviviparous animal that keeps eggs inside its body while they develop and hatch

parthenogenesis when an egg cell develops into a young animal without having been fertilized by a male. In reptiles, offspring produced in this way are always female.

pigment natural coloring of animals

plastron lower part of a tortoise or turtle shell

poaching hunting animals for their meat, skin, or shells

predator animal that catches and kills other animals

prehensile able to wrap around objects to grip them, such as the tail of a chameleon

prey animal that is killed and eaten by other animals

primitive at an early stage of evolution or development

reptile ectothermic, egg-laying vertebrate with tough, scaly skin

respiration process of gas exchange that allows an animal to absorb oxygen and release carbon dioxide

scute scale that forms a covering on the outside of reptiles

skeleton bony framework of an animal

species group of individuals that share many characteristics and can interbreed to produce offspring

streamlined able to move through water easily

temperate mild climate with distinct seasons

terrestrial living on land

territory range or area claimed by an animal or group of animals

torpid inactive

tropical hot and wet climate

venom poison

vertebrate animal that has a backbone

viviparous giving birth to live young

Further Information

Fullick, Ann. *Ecosystems & Environment*. Chicago: Heinemann Library, 2000.

Parker, Edward. *Reptiles and Amphibians*. Chicago: Raintree, 2003.

Sachidhanandam, Uma. *Threatened Habitats*. Chicago: Raintree, 2004.

Spilsbury, Louise and Richard Spilsbury. *Classifying Reptiles*. Chicago: Heinemann Library, 2003.

Spilsbury, Richard. *Alligator*. Chicago: Heinemann Library, 2004.

Townsend, John. *Incredible Reptiles*. Chicago: Raintree, 2005.

Unwin, Mike. *The Life Cycle of Reptiles*. Chicago: Heinemann Library, 2003.

Index

agamids 42, 43
alligators 7, 16, 50–51, 54, 55
amphibians 4, 6, 60
amphisbaenians 7, 16, 17
anacondas 29, 31
anguids 47
aquatic reptiles 11, 12, 17, 18, 20, 22, 23, 24–25, 34, 35, 40, 46, 50–53

basking 11, 27, 52
beaks 5, 16, 20
boas 13, 15, 28, 29, 30–31, 55
burrowing reptiles 17, 27, 40, 45

camouflage 30, 31, 35, 39, 41
chameleons 12, 14, 41, 42–43, 60
chelonians 16, 18, 20–25, 60, 61
climbing reptiles 12, 17, 29, 30, 31, 32, 40, 41, 44, 45, 46, 60
cobras 29, 35, 36–37
color change 6, 11, 41, 42–43
colubrids 32–33
conservation 56–57
constriction 28, 29, 31, 33
crocodiles 7, 12, 16, 17, 50–53, 58
crocodilians 7, 11, 14, 16, 17, 19, 50–53, 55, 60, 61
    eggs and young 51, 52, 53
    food 50, 51, 52, 53

defense 29, 31, 33, 35, 36, 37, 38, 40, 43, 45
dinosaurs 18, 19, 60

ectothermy 4–5, 10, 59
eggs 4, 5, 6–7, 8, 9, 23, 24, 25, 27, 29, 31, 33, 34, 36, 39, 45, 47, 48, 51, 53, 56–57, 59
egg teeth 6, 9, 25, 48
elapids 34–37
estivation 10, 28
evolution 4, 6, 18–19, 23, 38, 58, 60–61
extinct reptiles 18–19, 26

eyelids 14, 17, 47
eyes 4, 14, 26, 44, 45, 50

fangs 29, 33, 34, 38, 59
fossils 18, 19, 20

geckos 4, 7, 10, 12, 13, 40, 44–45
gharials 50, 51, 56
Gila monsters 17, 40, 41, 47

habitats 4, 5, 6, 8, 10, 11, 17, 22, 23, 26, 27, 28, 30, 32, 33, 34, 36, 37, 38, 40, 42, 43, 44, 46, 47, 48, 50, 51, 52, 54, 56
hearing 14, 15, 29, 50
heat sensors 15, 29, 39
hibernation 8, 10, 28, 32

iguanas 11, 13, 42–43
incubation 8, 25, 47, 56

Komodo dragons 46, 48–49

life span 21, 27, 53
limbs 4, 5, 12, 17, 20, 40, 48
lizards 4, 5, 6, 7, 10, 11, 13, 14, 15, 16, 17, 19, 40–49, 54, 55, 59, 60
    eggs and young 45, 47, 48
    food 11, 17, 41, 42, 43, 45, 46, 47, 48, 49

mating 6, 8, 9, 23, 34, 35, 36, 48, 53
migration 23, 24
molting 7, 8, 9, 34, 39
monitor lizards 17, 40, 46–47, 53
movement 12–13, 16, 17, 19, 20, 23, 24, 28–29, 35, 40, 48, 50, 51

nictitating membrane 14, 50
nocturnal reptiles 4, 14, 27, 44–45

parental care 7, 8, 9, 23, 24, 25, 29, 31, 36, 45, 48, 52, 53

parthenogenesis 9, 45
poisonous reptiles 17, 29, 32, 33, 34–39, 40, 47, 49
pythons 9, 13, 15, 17, 29, 30–31, 55

rattlesnakes 9, 39

scales 4, 5, 12, 13, 26, 27, 28, 29, 32, 34, 44, 47, 50, 59
senses 14–15, 29, 39, 41, 48, 50
shells 5, 16, 20, 21, 22, 23, 24, 55, 57
sight 14, 29, 41, 48
skin 4, 5, 6, 18, 44, 55, 57, 59
skinks 7, 17, 45, 55
smell 14, 15, 48
snakes 5, 7, 8–9, 11, 13, 14, 15, 16, 17, 19, 28–39, 54, 55, 59, 60
    eggs and young 8–9, 29, 31, 33, 34, 35, 39
    food 15, 17, 28, 29, 31, 32, 33, 34, 35, 36
squamates 16, 17, 59, 60, 61
swimming reptiles 12, 20, 23, 24, 34, 35, 36, 50–53

tails 30, 39, 41, 45, 47, 60
teeth 20, 41, 42, 49, 50, 51
temperature 6, 8, 10–11, 22, 24, 25, 27, 28, 32, 52
terrapins 20–25
tortoises 5, 7, 14, 16, 18, 20–25, 55, 56–57
tree-dwelling reptiles 30, 31, 32, 34, 40, 42, 44, 45, 46, 48, 60
tuataras 7, 11, 14, 16, 19, 26–27, 60, 61
turtles 5, 6, 12, 13, 14, 16, 18, 19, 20–25, 54, 55, 56–57, 58

venom 17, 29, 33, 34, 35, 36, 38, 47, 59
vipers 15, 38–39, 59

young 5, 6, 7, 9, 20, 21, 23, 25, 27, 29, 31, 33, 35, 36, 39, 45, 48, 52, 53